BUILD SOCIAL CONFIDENCE

*Maximize Your Likability,
Connect To People Instantly,
Handle Tough Conversations With
Courage*

Zoe McKey

Communication Coach and
Social Development Trainer

zoemckey@gmail.com
www.zoemckey.com

Copyright © 2017 by Zoe McKey. All rights reserved.

No part of this publication may be reproduced, stored in a retrieval system, or transmitted in any form or by any means, electronic, mechanical, photocopying, recording, scanning or otherwise, except as permitted under Section 107 or 108 of the 1976 United States Copyright Act, without the prior written permission of the author.

Limit of Liability/ Disclaimer of Warranty: The author makes no representations or warranties with respect to the accuracy or completeness of the contents of this work and specifically disclaims all warranties, including without limitation warranties of fitness for a particular purpose. No warranty may be created or extended by sales or promotional materials. The advice and recipes contained herein may not be suitable for everyone. This work is sold with the understanding that the author is not engaged in rendering medical, legal or other professional advice or services. If professional assistance is required, the services of a competent professional person should be sought. The author shall not be liable for damages arising herefrom. The fact that an individual, organization of website is referred to in this work as a citation and/or potential source of further information does not mean that the author endorses the information the individual, organization to website may provide or recommendations they/it may make. Further, readers should be aware that Internet websites listed in this work might have changed or disappeared between when this work was written and when it is read.

For general information on the products and services or to obtain technical support, please contact the author.

Thank you for choosing my book! I would like to show my appreciation for the trust you gave me by giving **FREE GIFTS** for you!

For more information visit: www.zoemckey.com

The checklist talks about *5 key elements of building self-confidence* and contains extra actionable worksheets with practice exercises for deeper learning.

Learn how to:
- Solve 80% of you self-esteem issues with one simple change
- Keep your confidence permanent without falling back to self-doubt
- Not fall into the trap of promising words
- Overcome anxiety
- Be confident among other people

The cheat sheet teaches you three key daily routine techniques to become more productive, have less stress in your life, and be more well-balanced. It also has a step-by-step sample sheet that you can fill in with your daily routines.

Discover how to:
- Overcome procrastination following 8 simple steps
- Become more organized
- Design your yearly, monthly, weekly and daily tasks in the most productive way.
- 3 easy tricks to level up your mornings

Table of Contents

INTRODUCTION	11
CHAPTER 1: INSIDE OUT	19
CHAPTER 2: WHY PEOPLE FEAR SOCIAL INTERACTIONS?	29
CHAPTER 3: EVERYONE'S FAVORITE TOPIC	41
CHAPTER 4: THREE THINGS THAT RUIN A CONVERSATION	49
CHAPTER 5: HOW TO BUILD CHARISMA	57
CHAPTER 6: THE POWER OF NO	71
CHAPTER 7: BE SELFISH	77
CHAPTER 8: LEAVE THE PAST IN THE PAST	87

CHAPTER 9: CONVERSATION CHAMELEON — 93

CHAPTER 10: HOW TO HANDLE DIFFICULT CONVERSATIONS — 103

CHAPTER 11: BE TOUGH INSTEAD OF RUDE — 111

CHAPTER 12: RESPECT MUST BE EARNED — 117

CHAPTER 13: DEEPEN AND OPEN — 124

CHAPTER 14: FIFTY POINTS OF SOCIAL CONFIDENCE — 133

EPILOGUE — 138

MORE BOOKS BY ZOE — 140

Introduction

Is there someone who you'd desperately want to impress? Your boss, your platonic love, the fussy saleslady at your local grocery store?

When finally you are face to face with *that* person and you feel your big moment is here, you take a deep breath, and …

… You can't say a word. You just awkwardly gape like a fish and then change your walking direction. You try to pretend that you were just yawning and made a wrong turn when you stopped in front of her with all your might. *"Did she buy it? I hope she did … Can it go any worse than this?"* Actually, it can.

What's worse than saying nothing is saying way too much. You blab and blab, and somewhere in the course of the blabbing, you lose your point because you're very nervous. You realize this, you block for a second, and when you catch the tail of your "cool story," you resume blabbing. In the meantime, the subject of your interest looks right through you with an unimpressed face, chewing bubblegum.

Suddenly you realize that you said some very weird stuff. Words can't be withdrawn, my friend. What's out is out.

Don't worry. We've all been there, even the cool person who you wish to impress so desperately. Social bloopers happen. If, however, you think you experience more bloopers than those around you, or your life is a constant blooper-to-blooper road, you have to put in extra effort if you want to change. But you can change. And you should.

Why?

Because being socially fluent, likable, and charming are maybe the most important skills ever. Your entire life orbits around different social interactions — friendships, relationships, companionships, work relations etc. If you can't communicate what you want charmingly enough to a possible partner, intriguingly enough to a possible friend, or succinctly enough to a possible business partner, you'll be left behind.

During my career as a coach, I met many kinds of people who had communication difficulties. You may think that these people were born in front of the computer, blind on one side, missing their noses, wearing Roman togas, and oozing awkwardness from each pore. Wrong. Most people who struggle with social confidence have their stuff together otherwise. They have nice personalities, good jobs ... Sometimes I was startled and wondered, *Why does this person need communication coaching?*

When we started talking, I slowly put the picture together. When I asked them what day should be good for the next session, they would start talking about their dog shedding more than usual. When I asked when the dog last saw a vet, they replied, "Wednesday." Their responses were full of bad timing, randomness, and long, weird silences.

Some people say, "But I have great values, I have so much to give." I'm sure you do. You can have the greatest personality in the world, but if you can't share it with others effectively, you won't be able to build good relationships.

Do you often feel like you're the person who always stands in the corner at a gathering? The one nobody cares about? The one who came because the crazy friend dragged you to the party, only to ditch you in search of cooler people? You are the one in the gray shirt, awkwardly holding a Solo cup of beer and bopping your head to the rhythm of the music to pretend you're having fun.

On the outside you seem ... chill? But inside, your head is full of chaos. All your brain cells are in emergency preparedness mode and on high alert to be able to answer questions like, "How do you do?" and "What's your name?"

Odds are against you being asked a question that requires an answer of more than three words — including *hi*. And here comes that girl in the blue dress, she's approaching, very close ...

She's going to talk to me. What should I do?

Your inner alarm beeps loudly in your head, your heart rate rises to at least two thousand and clears the thoughts from your mind. You go completely blank. And suddenly … she changes direction and enters the restroom. You feel relieved and disappointed at the same time.

The biggest obstacles in front of people who are not fluent in social interaction are the following two convictions:

That charisma and social fluency is something that the lucky ones are simply "born with."

That social interaction must be learned and thought through logically.

These beliefs are wrong. Conversations are creative exercises. The skills one needs to have good conversations, therefore, are not the skills of the logical, thinking brain. Good conversation skills need the training of the emotional brain. Just think about the stereotype of mathematicians and IT people ("geeks"); they tend to have a bad reputation when it comes to social fluency. Why? Because they try to be too logical. Social interactions can be practiced and improved upon just like anything else in this world. You're not born with the skill of flipping pancakes with one hand or speaking Chinese, either. No one is born as an absolutely talented conversationalist, and no one is born to be absolutely weak in it.

There is a habit I learned in my chaotic, always-on-the-move teenage years and have applied ever since. When I go somewhere completely unknown, I do my research beforehand. Being flawless in social situations is often a matter of comfortable knowledge. If you know something for sure, you're less likely to feel weird talking about it, whereas when you feel that you know nothing about the person or culture, but you wish to fill the space with words anyway, that's when bloopers happen. If you want to learn something, you have to do your research. If you want to hang out with boxers, for example, check out Wikipedia at least and upgrade your knowledge about this sport. You won't become a master of the topic, but you'll be able to add to the conversation — at least in form of questions.

If you want to make a very good impression, talk with somebody about the interests and habits of the group you want to join. Talking to one person under casual circumstances is less scary and can help you become well-informed. Maybe you'll have to push yourself if you fear talking to new people, but you have to start somewhere. And how can you do it with less discomfort than in front of only one human? It will help a great deal if you already know your questions so the only thing you have to do is ask them. Who can this person be? Anyone, really. If we want to stick to the example of boxing, go to a bar close to a boxing ring and talk to the bartender while sipping a beer. Hey, minors, no alcohol for you, eh?

Another lesson I've learned early in life is that we have two ears and only one mouth, so we should listen twice as much as we speak. Good listening skills often matter more than good communication skills when you want to make a good impression. Listen to what others are saying, and when you find the right moment, jump into the conversation.

A few years ago, I spent three months in a city where I didn't know anybody. I went to the local gym to work out and socialize. When I hit the sauna, two people, a boy and a girl, were talking about mosquitos invading the forests nearby. When I heard about the mosquitos, I felt my time has come to say something. I showed them the huge mosquito bite on my forearm, telling them I knew what they meant. I was camping just a day ago near the forest and the mosquitos killed me. They swiftly nodded, then asked where I came from and the conversation started rolling. We are friends to this day. Mosquitos can make you life-long friends, just saying.

Being a gray mouse in conversations is natural. Staying a gray mouse is a decision. Everybody is interesting; everybody has a story to tell in a way nobody else can. Good conversations can be broken down to two skills: understanding and relating to the thoughts and emotions expressed by others, and fluently expressing thoughts and emotions yourself.

The goal of this book is to help improve your verbal comprehension, thought organization, confidence, empathy, listening skills, and social courage by focusing on each of them individually and assigning you exercises so you can practice them.

Chapter 1: Inside Out

Guitar lessons, chemical experiments, dancing, chess — what do these things have in common? Seemingly nothing, so I will tell you: It is commonly accepted that with practice, one can improve and get better in the aforementioned activities. You learn and practice, you improve; you don't learn and practice, you don't improve. The skill mastery curve is this simple.

However, for some reason when it comes to social conversations and fluency, people commonly hold a different belief: that some are born to be socially likable, and some aren't. And with that, the less socially fluent people give themselves over to fate and never try to get better. They accept that they are bad at social stuff.

Socializing is just like any other skill — it has to be practiced and learned in order for you to get better at it. Just like with any other skill, there are those one-in-a-million geniuses who were born with a higher aptitude for socializing than others. This doesn't mean that regular folks can't learn to socialize just as well, or even better than those with a natural talent for it. It just requires work.

And as we know, people tend to shy away from hard work. In the short-term, it seems easier to convince ourselves that we are not good at socializing, or any other activity that requires effort to change. Here are some examples of the self-deceiving beliefs we feed ourselves every day:

I can't quit smoking. I've always been a smoker. I can't do it. I've always been a quitter. I am bad at conversations. I can't speak to people easily.

Sound familiar? The problem with these self-deceptive negative thoughts is that they become self-fulfilling prophecies. You know why? Because you believe them. I can't count how many of these iron-clad beliefs people construct and follow every day. I could also call them excuses. Or I could call them things that need to be changed, but the only way to change is through hard work.

I don't want to lie to you. You may never become the greatest orator, speaker, or charmer who ever lived if you read and respect the tips in this book. But I can promise you that if you take only a few bits of advice and practice them diligently, in a few months or years, you will become a much better conversationalist than you are today.

People think in extremes. The best or the worst. People think in comparisons. Better than he or she. The first thing you should realize that self-improvement is only about you and no one else. The sole goal here is to get better than a day before. So don't worry, and don't fall prey to fears. You can't go wrong if you try to improve in one way or another. The only wrong way is doing nothing to change the things you feel uncomfortable with.

There is nothing wrong with having flaws — everybody has them, and indeed, that makes us human. Talking about our weaknesses can help our social situation just as much as it can hurt it. How?

Our vulnerability is our armor. But vulnerability is only attractive when it pairs up with courage. If you confess a weakness against your fears, it will come off as a demonstration of strength and gutsiness. For example, if you tell people that you often feel insecure about how to start a conversation, but you are doing your best to overcome it, many will sympathize with you, relate to your issue, and admire you for being honest and open. If you present your vulnerability in a complaining, attention-seeking way, people will feel drained by you. The same weakness can be used as a weapon — it depends on you whether it is a weapon that raises you up, or becomes one of self-destruction.

At the end of the day, nobody will remember your words. People will remember how you made them feel. If they feel inspired and charged, they will want to connect with you more. But if people feel drained by your constant complaining, they will avoid you.

Let people like you for who you are.

If you always say what you think others want to hear, you'll never experience true satisfaction in a conversation. You'll feel a strange gut-level squeeze because you know you didn't say what you wanted, and you won't achieve your goal of being more likable.

Find the cause of your self-destructive thoughts.

Is it because you lack self-confidence? Do you use forced incompetence as a coping mechanism? Or do you use self-pity as an excuse to stay inactive? Intentional self-harm is mentally and physically damaging. Here are some quick tips on how to rethink what to say and not say to yourself:

Don't say anything about yourself that you wouldn't say about your mother, your love, or your best friend. Every time you feel that negative train coming, ask yourself: *Would I say this about …?* If your answer is no, then you don't deserve the bad label, either.

Stop reading beauty magazines.

Researchers have shown that regular readers of beauty magazines have a much higher level of self-criticism. First, acknowledge that the perfect men and women on the pages are mostly Photoshopped. Then realize that those people cultivate their beauty for a living. They are not busy lawyers, tired nurses, or full-time stay-at-home mothers. Why read something that makes you feel ugly? Social acceptance and respect do not come from beauty, but from an overall stable and reliable personality.

Are introverts all shy?

These days there is a clear misunderstanding of what introversion is. When someone is labeled to be an introvert, the word is usually used to emphasize the person's inaptness to be social. The word seems to be a synonym for shyness and social withdrawal. This interpretation is wrong. Introverts draw their energy from being alone, while extroverts draw their energy from being around people. That's it. Introversion doesn't mean that someone is socially inapt.

I would be surprised if you thought Johnny Depp, Barack Obama, or Bill Gates are socially awkward. Yes, they are all introverts.

Introversion is not a weakness or a problem. Social anxiety is the true problem which affects both extroverts and introverts. Social anxiety makes extroverts talk more and introverts talk less. Shyness is the companion of introverts who are socially anxious.

Introversion is an innate personality trait that one can't change and shouldn't aim to. Shyness and social anxiety, on the other hand, can be changed — with hard work and dedication, they can be improved.

In conventional thinking, extroversion is cool and introversion is lame. That's bollocks. Neither one of these traits is better than the other. The person in question just naturally excels at different skills. As a shy introvert, you shouldn't aim to become an extrovert. Just aim to be more socially confident and capable of being talkative when a situation calls for it.

I'm a rational thinker. Can I be entertaining?

Yes, you can.

As I mentioned in the introduction, good communication is not a question of rationality, but rather, creativity. The dynamics of communication depend on how quickly and effectively can one draw associations between seemingly disparate events or topics and present them with a unique angle. For example, seeing an animal that resembles a publicly hated figure, making the association, and sharing the resemblance with others packaged into a funny sentence can break any ice.

People who are more creative by nature can find these associations quickly and effortlessly. Their brain is tuned for humor and they have an associative world view. Others are structured, linear thinkers. For them, seeing these seemingly illogical connections is really challenging. They have to put in extra effort to learn creative associative thinking — nevertheless, they can learn it.

The other deal breaker skill one should develop to be more socially likable (apart from creative association) is emotional awareness. This emotional awareness should be bidirectional: awareness of one's own feelings, and awareness of the feelings of others, at the same time. Just like at any other skill, some people are born to be more emotionally perceptive. Some people are emotionally perceptive and empathetic by nature. Others are not so good at it.

Emotional perceptiveness, just like any other skill, can be improved through conscious effort.

There is an unwritten law of emotions: Relationships are going to get as good as one's ability to understand and react to others' emotions. But generally, one can't react and connect with people's emotions more than with his or her own.

Some people are more emotional than others. They can feel certain emotions stronger and understand others deeper than those who have repressed their emotional development for one reason or another. Women are said to be more emotionally perceptive in general. Men are encouraged to be and act rationally; they don't fall "prey" to their emotions.

People who can't empathize with others or their own emotions tend to have more shallow relationships than those who are emotionally well-wired. Developing emotional self-awareness and general awareness is a cornerstone to building good, profound relationships.

Who are you? An introvert or extrovert? Shy? Do you feel creative in your conversations? Are you a rational thinker? What about your emotional intelligence? Can you catch up on how people really feel, read between their words, or do you struggle with understanding your own emotions?

In the next chapters, you will find answers on how to improve any weaknesses you may think you have now.

Chapter 2: Why People Fear Socia Interactions?

Am I good enough? I am sure she will do better on the evaluation because she is smarter. Oh, why can't I be like her?

He is so good with words; everybody is hanging on his every utterance. I will never attract that much attention.

Familiar thoughts? You meet them at every corner. You meet with comparison from an early age. The most common comparisons that might affect you are those you hear from your parents or close relatives.

> - Why aren't you helping me more like Susan's daughter? Why aren't you studying as hard as your brother?

The example above is a very direct way of comparing, but there is another kind, the nasty, skin-ripping kind that we also often meet.

> - Oh, why do I deserve this? What have I done to earn such a never-do-well wife and dumb kids? What will happen to the business if …

In this sentence, the subject of comparison wasn't mentioned. Growing up in an environment where you can never be good enough will leave deep conscious and unconscious imprints on your future self-esteem. Negative comparisons suffered during childhood are a common underlying cause for a person's lack of social confidence.

Anxiety over not being good enough is very difficult to overcome. Even if you get over it on the surface — say you become fortunate and respected by society — when you go home and face that you are still not enough for your mother or not as good as your sister, those deep-rooted wounds split open, making you feel miserable and insignificant. Not enough. And your well-rehearsed mask instantly falls apart, leaving you with the bitter feeling of inadequacy.

What can you do? Difficult question. Difficult because people's experiences in this regard are various. The common thing is that they all have the same root: fear. Remember Yoda?

"Fear is the path to the dark side. Fear leads to anger. Anger leads to hate. Hate leads to suffering."

It is one of my favorite *Star Wars* quotes. You see, not only do I think it is true, but so does a Jedi master. And a Jedi master knows a thing or two about human nature.

So what are people usually afraid of? The unknown. In your case, the undiscovered part is your soul, values, and skills. Here we go again — know thyself. Or the unknown is simpler than that — we just don't remember what negative events triggered our social anxiety. Whatever happened in your childhood, most likely you don't remember the exact moment, words, or actions that made you socially fearful.

The triggers and the consequences vary widely from person to person. You might be okay with meeting new people, but fear to develop a deeper connection with them. Your neighbor might fear meeting new people, but once he gets familiar with them, his social anxiety vanishes. Some get socially anxious when they have to prove themselves — in a competition, a job interview, a public speech. All these are rooted in one big, or many small, past instance of negative conditioning.

You can't erase them. They are like spoken words, out there in the ether. But you can rewrite them with time. Question your anxious beliefs.

Did someone else criticize you? Look objectively at your critics. Are they reliable sources?

You know the saying — those who are positive about themselves don't criticize; they teach and inspire. Your critics might be people struggling with even more severe social anxiety than you are. People who have spent enough time in the "shadows of lack of self-esteem" tend to expand their acidity on those around them. Sometimes they are not even consciously doing so; they just do it because that's what they saw, or how they were treated before.

If you think it over, you'll realize there is no point in your getting upset because the whole story isn't about you. It is about them; their fears, rage, and inability to handle their anxieties. But if you feel your critics are right about what they say, accept it. Not because they said so, or because you want to match their expectations, but because you realized there is an area where you can improve.

Do you accept the criticism of your brother being better at handling his anger to be true? Find the reason why your brother is handling anger better than you. What does he do or have that you don't? Then think about how you can improve yourself based on what you observe.

If you realize and accept that somebody is better than you at something, instead of giving in to envy and fear, you choose to improve yourself to their level, and that's called growth. You used the power of comparison in a positive way. This is a big step.

What is social anxiety, exactly?

It is a self-constructed expectation where you wish to live up to something, but at the same time, you believe you're not good enough to do it.

For example, maybe you have a budget improvement proposal for your company. On one hand, you wish to boost your company's success greatly with your idea, but at the same time, you're not sure your plan is good enough.

If you present your plan and it turns out to be successful, you won't feel so anxious the next time. The more you repeat doing something, the less anxiety you'll feel about it. If your plan isn't a breakthrough success at first, but you don't give up and work on improvements, then the more you practice, the better you'll become.

Two things should you target to achieve: lower your expectations, and work on becoming more confident that your skills are sufficient to meet your expectations.

Let's put socially anxious introverts and extroverts under a microscope. As I said in the previous chapter, introverts tend to say nothing when they are anxious. They fear they might say something ridiculous. Extroverts, on the other hand, would blab from dusk to dawn, making sure not to leave any detail out of their conversation (monologue).

If you think these reactions through, they're both rooted in perfectionism. The introvert wants to sound perfect — if he has to say something. The extrovert doesn't want to seem uninteresting by not talking enough.

Both of them are busy with different distractions. Introverts are good at listening to others, but they fail to reconcile with their own selves. Extroverts are good at expressing themselves, but the fail to take others' emotions into consideration. They are not good listeners.

Social anxiety drives us to become utterly self-absorbed and obsessed with perfection. We stay so much in our heads that we fail to understand what people try to tell to us, or we fail to properly communicate our feelings and thoughts to others.

What can we do?

Nothing. Sorry. Nothing besides accepting that there will be times when we'll look silly, make word bloopers, and people will laugh about us. Other times, we will come through as obnoxious and people will not agree with us.

As good of a conversationalist you might become, you still are human who makes mistakes. Sometimes your bloopers are not even mistakes just general difference of opinion. You can't satisfy everybody. Stuff happens. You're not perfect, I'm not perfect — no one is.

There is no smart way around this block. You can list your good and bad qualities and recite them in front of a mirror, but you won't get the confidence you're looking for. You'll be more confident if you get out, practice, and accept that sometimes your conversation will suck. You're not a machine. As soon as you let go of your expectation of perfection, you suddenly will become more carefree and less anxious about your likability.

Sometimes it is better to say something stupid than say nothing at all, my introverted friend. Sometimes it is better to talk less and listen a bit, and you'll be expressive enough even so, my extroverted amigo. There's nothing wrong with you.

Lowered expectations are liberating. I don't mean not to have expectations at all, but don't aim for perfection and absolute certainty — those will never happen.

What can you do in practice?

Crush Emotional Spasms

What generates these spasms? Some people fear showing their true selves because they fear rejection. So they put on masks and pretend to be strong, self-assured, and confident, when in reality, they aren't. Behind these spasms — or we could call it ego — there is low self-esteem and a profound hunger for love.

How does a person without spasms act? A person who is okay internally is quick to smile (not a tormented grin but a sincere, heartfelt smile), laid-back, and spontaneous. People like this can straighten their backs. But there is hard work behind it.

How do you get rid of emotional spasms? First, you have to say this out loud:

I have spasms. Or, *I have trouble with this and that.*

Speak about it. It's a general misconception that if you talk about your problems, you're weak. Some think strength means silently carrying one's burdens, but this is incorrect.

To overcome a fear, you have to find words for it and say them out loud. If you don't speak of it in an effort to satisfy others' expectations, you won't help yourself. Admitting your fears and weaknesses is a sign of strength. If you admit one, you'll get rid of one spasm. If you admit to it, but don't change it, your problems will only deepen. So admit your fears and take clear, conscious action to address them.

Learn to be humble.

Ego and humbleness can't live together. Self-esteem and humbleness walk hand in hand. If you know you are good at something, that's a healthy condition. Boost your mood and performance with this strong belief. If you are good at something, why wouldn't you be proud of it?

Problems start when you start talking up your skills to others without being asked or simply for showing off. Then it becomes bragging and self-justification. It can also be a sign of overcompensation.

Bragging doesn't help you, anyway. If someone accepts that you are a good designer, for instance, will your self-appraisal make you a better designer? What if someone thinks you are a bad designer? You won't change their mind simply by telling them you're good. So why brag?

It is not boastful or defensive to share your excellence in a conversation when someone asks. Then say: *Yes, I'm good at layout design. What about you? What's your superpower?*

By telling the plain truth about yourself, then turning the focus back onto the other person, you give the impression you are straightforward and curious. Your conversation partner will be happy to get to talk about him or herself — people love that.

False modesty gets an F.

False modesty is unlikable. It is a passive way of bragging and can be displeasing. Remember the nerds in school? When you asked them how the test was and they replied it was awful, but then got the best score? When you feel inclined to be falsely modest, just think about the nerds in your class. Also, false modesty is a form of insecurity — you don't know how to receive compliments. Instead of sniggering awkwardly and denying the person's praise, just respond with a "counter compliment." Let's say somebody said you were a great designer. You reply:

Thanks, you have a sharp eye for quality.

This way you didn't deny your skills, yet you didn't seem over-confident either, like, *I know, right?*

Shut down your ego and grow your self-esteem.

Chapter 3: Everyone's Favorite Topic

Isn't it just easier to think something challenging won't work out, so why bother trying?

Have you already decided that you won't become good at social interactions? Would you rather keep headphones on your ears to avoid conversations? But while listening to music, are you daydreaming about being the soul of the community?

I bet you picture yourself being a great singer who is loved by many, living in another age, being successful and professionally admired, or being in a romantic relationship with Henry Cavill. Oh, yeah … Okay, time to step out of that fantasy world.

Good news! To some extent, all of these dreams can be achieved, but not by staying motionless. Being consciously antisocial, in addition to dooming yourself to a lonely life, is physically unhealthy.

According to research, loneliness can lead to several health diseases like stroke, depression, even suicide. So let's find the root of your antisocial behavior and cure it.

Stop being judgmental.

Self-proclaimed antisocial people have the tendency to frequently criticize themselves and those around them. They don't engage in social interaction because on one hand, they are afraid of being judged by others, and on the other hand, they judge other people. The difference between confident people and insecure people is the image they have of themselves.

Confident, sociable people focus on the positive qualities of those around them, as well as themselves. Unconfident, antisocial people tend to focus on their own deficiencies and the imperfections of others.

To stop this unhealthy way of thinking, make a list of your positive qualities. Include both emotional and physical characteristics. After making the list, be sure to remind yourself of it.

Stop labeling yourself as shy or antisocial. The more you have negative thoughts about yourself, the more you will reinforce this belief. If you constantly tell yourself you can't make social connections, guess what? You won't. But remember, all this mess is in your head, so it only depends on you. If you want to be more social, start by actually believing you can be.

Take action. "Do one thing every day that scares you." That's Eleanor Roosevelt's advice to you. In your case, this thing might be as simple as taking off your headphones and staying open to possible conversations. Listen to the sounds of nature, or to what people are talking about. It can be really interesting, and you'll realize that it's not that difficult to hold a casual conversation.

When you're comfortable enough being without headphones, take this exercise to the next level. Go and talk to people. Start with an innocent excuse like asking the time or for directions. When you are confident enough, try to get somebody's phone number or connect with them on Facebook. Whatever it is, just be uncomfortable. That's not a typo. Get out of the comfort zone of your unsocial habits. Don't be pushy or harass anyone; just be friendly when the situation allows it. Practice.

Believe that human nature is good. It is important to know that humans can be kind and accepting creatures. Isn't that a more encouraging approach when trying to meet new people?

Stop over-analyzing your interactions. Over-thinking social interactions is what hinders people from enjoying them. Although not easy, it is essential to break the habit of trying to predict what social engagements will be like before they happen. Also, stop over-analyzing your conversations word for word once they are over.

Approach every conversation with a positive attitude rather than focusing on how you would embarrass yourself and what could go wrong. Focus on the things that went well when the interaction is over instead of starting your analysis paralysis. Find a funny moment, new information you learned, or a thoughtful idea, even if the interaction itself wasn't that earth shaking.

Just like with any other skill, improving your social skills requires practice and persistence. It means you will have to get off the couch, get out of your comfort zone, and interact with people on a regular basis. After a while, it won't be a matter of demand, but a natural part of your day.

Everyone's favorite topic is ...

Themselves. That's right. Dale Carnegie rightfully pointed this out in his famous book, *How to Win Friends and Influence People*. Steering the conversation to the other party doesn't equal asking questions relentlessly. A plethora of questions can fill any conversation with a sense of interrogation instead of a pleasant exchange of ideas. The interaction becomes uneven and unbalanced.

You can show interest in the other party by peppering some statements between your questions. For example:

"So, did you like your last date?"
"I never thought he was your type of guy."
"Oh, where did you go for drinks?"
"Nice, I love it when men are that thoughtful. I bet you were charmed so much."
"Was the service kind at the bar?"
"I can see why you felt a bit off after such a plain service."
"I assume you won't go back there. When will you meet Mr. Thoughtful again?"

As you can see, the conversation orbits around the other person without constant question marks. People can and will react just as well to statements too. This way, the chat won't become a one-sided interrogation.

Keep emotions in the spotlight and facts backstage when you have a casual conversation.

Why?

Simply because people can relate to emotions much more than to facts. Facts are boring. Even if they are interesting, people can't relate to them. If you want to capture someone's attention, you'll do it through their soul, not their overburdened brain. The easiest way to stay on the emotional side is to explore the "whys" in your statement, not the "whats."

For example, your statement is that you didn't like San Francisco because it was dirty.

This is how the conversation looks like if you lead it through facts:

"I went to San Francisco for a holiday. It is such a dirty city. The number of homeless people is very high there. It's said to be the second dirtiest city in the US after..."

This is the emotional presentation:

"I didn't like San Francisco so much. I really tried, but when I accidentally stepped onto a rotten cabbage left in the middle of the street, I felt a bit off about the idea of walking all day. I had to buy new shoes. I saw so many weird things dropped on the street not far from the city center. Some streets smelled like my cat's litter box after I fed her tuna."

The example serves just for the sake of illustrating my point. I actually love SF.

It's much more interesting to talk about a topic through your own emotional filter than it is to present the topic based on the plain facts. This doesn't mean that you have to become mushy and gushy about the things you talk about, expressing an irrevocable emotional opinion about everything. It simply means injecting your personality into plain facts. Personal relationships are made through connecting as people, after all.

If you feel that you are more of a fact checker and

talker, I can recommend a good exercise for you. Pick a topic which is fact-based. Got it? Now try to present it from a "why" angle. Talk about this factual topic with emotions.

The easiest way to do it is to talk about why do you like this topic, or why are you interested in it. If you can construct a conversation around this, you can approach your chosen topic from a different "why" angle. Like why do you think this topic is relevant, why is this topic helping others … You name it. Practice to get better in connecting through emotions.

Chapter 4: Three Things That Ruin A Conversation

Top three problems that ruin your likability in conversations:

1. Compulsive compliance

Have you ever met somebody who was overly smarmy, trying too hard to please others?

"What's your favorite color?" you ask.
"Blue," replies the pleaser.
"Oh, cool, mine is green."
"Now that you mention it, I think mine is too."

This is a simplistic example, but you get the gist. Some people are overly compliant. They are so afraid of social rejection or are otherwise absorbed in the feeling of inadequacy that they can change their opinion about things as irrelevant as their favorite color — or movie, or music, or hobby ... The worst part is that they easily shift their values and sense of self just to try to fit in.

2. Being the expert all the time

The other way of overdoing your conversations is to act as if you're an expert in everything. Let's say there is a person who you just met. You walk together in the room when you see a painting on the wall. You express your admiration to the host:

"What a lovely picture!" you say.
Your companion quickly adds, "That's an early Impressionist painting from 1870s France."
"How do you know that?" you ask.
"I've been studying art forever. It's pretty basic information." He shrugs with a smug face.

You find his behavior a bit prissy, but you choose not to bother with arguing. Maybe the guy is an expert, indeed. But just the next moment when the host's cat sneaks into the room, your conversation partner raises his voice.

"That's a Burman-Siamese mix, six weeks old."
"How do you know that?" you ask again.

"I've been working with cats for twenty years."

At this point, you decide that your conversation partner is a narcissistic busybody who likes expressing his knowledge superiority each time he sees an occasion. Acting like your conversation partner is highly unlikable.

Trying to compulsively impress people won't make you likable. You don't have to play dumb either. Just don't show too much of your skills, knowledge, and charm in a short period of time unless you're at a job interview. Less is more when it comes to human communication. Also remember people like to talk about themselves, so if you are constantly dragging the attention onto yourself, others may not like you so much for that.

Think about what you think of people who are constantly trying to impress or please others. You probably put them somewhere between lame and obnoxious. If you think like this about others, how do you suppose others feel about you if you do similar things?

Instead of brainstorming about how to impress or comply with people, think about why you feel the need to please, imitate, or outsmart them. Do you consider them superior? Do you consider yourself superior?

None of these notions are good. Measure yourself on your terms, not others'. Do you still have the list of your good qualities? Look at them and think about how you could maximize your strengths for your own benefit while remaining socially likable at the same time. Remember, less is often more in conversation, especially if you just met somebody. If you want to be socially likable, apply the two ears, one mouth rule. Always apply it to yourself. Just think about how you feel if you are not allowed to add to the conversation. It feels bad, right? So learn from others' mistakes and do better.

3. Blocking if a topic is not familiar

The third problem that can shut off conversations is silence. This is a very organic way of cutting conversations short. In some sense, this is the opposite problem the "experts" are facing. When I talk about unfamiliar topics, I don't mean scientific topics, but everyday topics like penguins or tornadoes — topics that are uncommon, but don't necessarily require specific scientific knowledge.

(When conversations do require specific knowledge, the best thing you can do is admit you know nothing about it and ask the expert for information.)

Elephants, the multiplication of ants, and *Star Wars*. What would you do with them? Freeze, or get over your temporary lack of knowledge and ... improvise?

Improvisation skills can be real deal breakers in conversations. You never know what topic will come up next. You can't be prepared for everything. If you want to minimize the frequency of awkward silences, you should start strengthening your improvisation muscles.

How?

Create one hundred cards of different topics. On each card put one word. Random ones. Go online, open an article on Facebook, and write the tenth word in the article on the paper. You can ask your family members and friends to help you come up with words.

When you have a word on each card, shuffle them like a normal deck and pick one. Speak about the word on the card for one to one and a half minutes without stopping.

This is a creativity exercise. It doesn't focus on facts. What's your word? "Hiking"? Talk about hiking as creatively as possible. For example: you could talk about your latest hiking adventure, hiking movies like *Wild*, or even hitchhiking. You can talk about what the dangers are of hiking alone, at night, or what the top three places you'd like to go hiking are. What are the alternative activities you'd rather do if you hate hiking? You can choose anything.

The only goal is to keep up your monologue for sixty to ninety seconds. You can brainstorm questions you'd ask your conversation partner about hiking, too.

Repeat this exercise ten times a day. It requires ten to fifteen minutes of your time, but it will help you a lot with quick thinking and improvising. Don't put back the cards you've already used to avoid picking the same words the next day. When you finish off your one hundred-word deck, create new word cards. Mix together the old and the new cards and go on with this exercise until you get comfortable with improvising.

Don't forget about the emotional impact of the conversation. Remember, people can connect to emotions more than facts. Talk about why do you love or hate hiking. Share your beliefs and opinions about the word on the paper.

Chapter 5: How to Build Charisma

What is charisma? It's such an appealing word, right? And I bet when you say it, someone charismatic instantly pops into your mind. For me, that person is the ex-foreign minister of Hungary. I know, politicians — it may seem cliché, but ...

Here's the short version of my experience: I studied foreign policy in college, and I participated in a competition in which the main prize was to spend an afternoon with the foreign minister. Each university that taught foreign policy sent their best students to the event, and I was one of the lucky ones among them.

I expected him to be an overconfident, boastful type of person who wouldn't give a few undergraduate students the time of day. Or he'd be utterly boring and lame, drooling all through the meeting, wondering, "Why do I have to be here?" But when I met him, my negative preconceptions vanished instantly.

He had an everyman persona, which in the beginning seemed fake, but as the afternoon wore on I started to feel less and less sure. He was so direct and likable. He told me he played the piano and I told him I did too, and we imitated a virtual duet together. He told me some stories of his youth and his work years where he used his piano skills to grab people's attention. Well, his stories totally captured me. I felt like we could be buddies.

The only word I could think of to describe him was — charismatic. "Is this how charisma looks and feels?" I thought.

I still find it difficult to describe what he did, but I know how he made me feel. Even with twelve other students, teachers, politicians, and a bodyguard in the room, he made me feel like I was his sole focus. He ignored everybody else when he was talking to me, maintained eye contact, and casually asked me personal and thoughtful questions I didn't expect. What's more, he actually seemed to care about my answers.

He probably didn't, but the empathy he exuded was so heartwarming it made me feel important and interesting.

So I thought, *Why doesn't everybody increase their charisma and use it in everyday life?* It creates warmth, interest, and happiness in the recipient's mind.
So what is charisma again? It's hard to define the concept itself, but it's easy to say what you want to achieve with it. It boosts your likability instantly with little effort. If you are charismatic, people will want to be around you so you can make them feel special. I would say that if you are charismatic, you're not a people-pleaser, but you are pleasing people.

Charisma means presence. It doesn't necessarily mean that when you step into a room everybody looks at you, but it means you are engaged in what's happening around you. Charisma can be learned. If I can believe anything the ex-foreign minister said, he used to be a withdrawn, shy, and self-conscious young man. In his late fifties, he was many things, but not shy or awkward. Charisma is not a question of innate ability, but of practice.

How can you develop charisma and use it with

confidence?

The first step

Put away your phone and be present when you are among people. With social media you miss out, and people may think you aren't interested. You seem distant, as if you'd rather be somewhere else. If you're present, you can be intensely curious and get to know as much as possible about those around you.

Become an engaging storyteller

In the previous chapters, I highlighted that humans can relate to emotions more so than to facts. Do you know how can you harness the most of the human ability to relate? If you present the emotions through stories.

Just think about how engaged you become when you watch a good story on TV. A documentary or a movie about a war triggers much deeper and more powerful emotions in you than the news about the same war does. Why? Because the news presents the plain facts. Stories go beyond that. Your soul gets touched when survivors speak up, presenting the horrific events through their own filter, telling you the true story of their life.

For example, I always heard that in the confection industry, millions of people get exploited in Southeast Asia, working in horrible conditions, getting just a few cents as an hourly wage. Living or dying, doesn't matter — the wheel goes on. Whenever I hear about this in the news or from others I feel sorry, but it's never really touched me. One day I saw a Netflix documentary where they presented the life and struggle of a woman working in a big clothing factory in Bangladesh. I clung onto each minute of that documentary. Seeing the horrors with my own eyes, feeling the sadness and helplessness of that woman and her family, triggered something in me. Since then, I've completely changed my clothes shopping habits. I choose to support a few small American manufacturers who produce their products in the US, paying fair wages to their workers. I completely stopped shopping at the mass market brands whose tags proudly state "Made in Indonesia" or "Made in Bangladesh." Now I know what it means, and I don't want to partake in these companies' crimes.

I don't want to shift your fashion ideas; I only talked about this particular moment of my life to prove to you the tremendous power well-presented stories have over us.

They don't have to be sad stories. Comedies, romances — they all have the same effect. They touch us. No wonder that throughout history, word-of-mouth stories have survived in the form of legends, anthems, and heroic tales.

"Great, but I don't have any good stories to tell," you may say. Let me assure you, even the most boring, everyday events can have a good story angle. The emphasis is not on what you tell, but how you tell it.

Good stories usually follow a definitive structure. The secret of good storytelling is following this structure fairly well. Each good story has three main parts: a setup, a conflict, and a resolution.

The setup gives us a glimpse into the stage where the story occurs. For example, "It was a rainy afternoon." The conflict brings a tension, an unpredictable event, into the picture. For example, "The dark figure followed me into the shadowy alley still soaked by the rain."

The resolution dissolves the tension and unpredictability, bringing peace after the uncertainty caused by the conflict. For example, "The dark figure was my best friend running after me in a giant black raincoat, bringing me my phone that I left at his place."

The resolution brings closure to the uncertainty and unleashes the tension caused by the first two parts of the story — e.g., "It turned out she was faking, so I hit her with a pillow for scaring me so much."

There are some unwritten laws considering the length of the parts of the story. The setup shouldn't be too long, otherwise you'll lose your audience's attention. If you talk too much about the green fields, or about the clothing details of the main characters, your audience's attention will wander away. I don't know about you, but as a kid, I always flipped through the pages where the author described the surroundings. "I don't care about how many hummingbirds sang on the old oak tree. Bring me to the point at once," I thought. In spoken language, it is better to keep the setup as short and simple as possible.

The conflict can be as long or short as you wish. The emphasis here is on creating uncertainty, doubt, dilemma, and a hint of danger. In many cases, this is not an easy task. Some conflicts have to be well-explained so the reader understands why the twist or dilemma is indeed meaningful. For example, if you say, "Greg didn't get accepted into the car race, so he wandered to a bridge, maybe with the thought of ending his life," the reader might say Greg is silly, he can try again, it's just one rejection. But if you elaborate on how Greg tried to get into this competition for ten years, how his dad got crippled at work so he can help his son achieve his dream, how Greg had his hopes up all this time, and how racing was his entire life, then the reader will understand that this failure is indeed serious. Greg wishing to end his life is not something random, but is rather the product of utter disappointment. This story is all about the conflict, about how Greg got up again and again during the years and tried harder than before each time.

Still, make sure to not extend the conflict part for too long. Any uncertainty can become boring if it is too detailed and lengthy. A vague or weak dilemma is also boring.

There are times when the conflict can be very short. For example, "And suddenly, the man in red pulled out a gun on the subway."

The resolution should be the shortest section of your story. This part should solve the conflict one way or another and it's supposed to prove a point, or tell a lesson. Otherwise, why should anyone waste time to listen to the story? For example, "Greg took a deep breath on the bridge and then suddenly threw his car keys into the water. He was done, he thought, and walked off in the sunset." Or, "The man in red turned out to be a private detective. He'd just caught a dangerous criminal on the subway."

If you feel that you are not a naturally gifted storyteller, don't worry. You can learn how to tell stories with captivating conflicts and great resolutions. You just have to practice.

Do you still have your card deck that you used to practice improvisation? Use them to practice storytelling, too. Pick a card and construct a story around the word on the card. At first the setup, the conflict, and the resolution can be one-liners. Then, when you feel more comfortable, start constructing longer, more captivating stories around the chosen words.

For example, you picked the word tornado.

The setup: "The news warned about a big tornado not far from us."
The conflict: "It turned out the tornado had changed direction and was heading directly toward our home."
The resolution: "Before causing any damage, the tornado changed direction again, narrowly avoiding our house."

You see? It is that simple. When you feel more comfortable, add emotions to this story. Talk about the fear, the sorrow you felt, how you started frantically collecting the mementos left behind by your dead grandmother, etc.

Appeal to people's perceived selves.

In other words, encourage them in what they seem interested in. For example, if somebody identifies with fitness, say that they are in a good shape and ask about their latest fitness routines. Stroke their ego. It is very important to be genuine. If somebody is not in shape, don't lie. That's not charismatic. That's dishonest. Find something you can truly appreciate in that person. If he is out of shape, but wears cool Nike sneakers, comment on them. The equation looks like this: Find something the person is interested in, figure out an honest compliment about the person in question relating to his interest, and say it to the person.

See, don't just look. Observe tiny changes people make so they can cash in on a compliment or two. When somebody has changed something about his or her appearance, make a kind remark and give a reassuring feedback. You'll be regarded as observant, and that person will want to open up to you and be nice to you in return.

Have a role model.

I don't mean you should imitate anybody, but I bet there is somebody in your life (be it someone you know personally, or a historic figure like Abraham Lincoln) whose lifestyle, attitude, and relationships with people attract you. Analyze this person's behavior and write down what specific things he or she did that you would like to "imitate." For example: *"I would like to have the accommodating temper or adaptive wit that she does."*

Then look at yourself. What do you lack? What prevents you from being like your role model? Do you lack an accommodating temper because you take everything seriously and get angry quickly? If this is the case, try to cultivate patience; count to eleven. If you are criticized unfairly, tell yourself that what you hear is not about you, but about the other person's insecurity. Think about how your role model would act in a similar situation.

Be the main and supporting actor at the same time.

The main character of a story is who gets the attention. He or she is attractive, charismatic, and everybody wants to emulate them. Well, here's the twist: If you want to be treated like a main character, you have to act like the supporting character. The supporting character is the one who cares about others, who is the pillar of the storyline, and who makes the main actor the center of attention.

In real life, if you give others attention as a supporting actor, others will consider you the main actor. Think about any movie where the protagonist is appreciated and supported by others — it's because the protagonist also cares about the supporting actors. The supporting players make the main actor the most important. This attitude creates a feedback loop. You act as the supporting actor to others, but others will perceive you as the main actor who is saving them. People don't like to feel indebted, so they pay you back with the same caring and supportive currency. Thus you'll feel like the main actor, as well. You have to be both at the same time — give and get.

It never works out for the anti-heroes who consider themselves to be the only ones they need. They only help themselves and don't accept help from others. Maybe they use others for their own purposes, but in the end, nobody will support them and they will fall. The hero is the hero because they save the world, not him or herself.

> "Become generally interested in other people."
> "Smile."
> "Make the other person feel important and do it sincerely."
> —Dale Carnegie

Chapter 6: The Power of No

Do you ever say no? Do you feel weird saying no to a friend or even a stranger? Are you buying everything that sellers push into your hands? If so, then you are in a bad relationship with the word "no."

It is a problem if you only say yes to save your skin from creating an awkward situation, like when you know that dress looks horrible on your friend. She asks for an honest opinion, and you lie in an effort not to offend her. There are many steps between a plain and unfriendly no and yes, yes, yes. You can point out that another dress fits her better, or refer to a particular trait of the dress, like the color, that you don't like.

Also, by always saying yes, you are making everyone else a priority instead of yourself. You tell yourself no so often, yet you struggle with saying it to others. Something's wrong with this, isn't it?

Say no for yourself.

You have the right to defend your life, your time, your opinions, and your values. When you feel that someone is trying to take advantage of your generosity, it is time to let them know that you know. You don't have to be rude about it. Simply tell them the time they suggested, let's say Monday, is not good because you already have something else planned. You will gladly help them on Tuesday when you are free. They can't get mad because you offered your help, and you just respected yourself and your schedule too. So it was a no, but it wasn't. If they still get mad and demand Monday, it means these people don't respect you or your plans. If that's the case, why should you help them in the first place?

If somebody asks you to do something you really wouldn't like to do — like, ever — because it opposes your values or you don't have the time, it may be best to tell them no more frankly. *I'm sorry, I won't do this because …* And give a short but explicit reason. If you're talking to a total stranger, you don't even have to give a reason. For a friend, it is better to add a short explanation. If the person is truly your friend, they'll understand. If they don't understand, then they are not worth being put before your interests anyway.

Prioritize.

All of us have twenty-four hours in a day, and most of us have a limited budget, so you have to prioritize who you say yes and no to. Surprisingly, many of my friends tend to say yes more often to strangers because they feel weird declining them, but to their friends and family, they say no easier.

It's less risky to say no to someone who loves you anyway, but consider how much value a stranger has in your life compared to your spouse or family member. I can only suggest making a priority list in your head and after satisfying your needs, put those who really matter at the top. Consider this — maybe it's more awkward to turn down a stranger, but you'll feel less bad afterwards. Meanwhile, saying no to your mom may haunt you even a week later. And you'll feel disappointed with yourself for doing it. Who needs those negative feelings?

Don't dispense your negative opinion unless you're asked.

Don't share your negative opinions unless you're asked about them. For example, don't go into a store and say to a random person, "Ugh, green's not your color." Be considerate even when you are asked.

If you are asked and you want to give an honest opinion, which in the given case is negative, do this first: Start with praise, then share your negative opinion indirectly. Speaking in third person is a good way to avoid delivering direct criticism.

For example, let's say your friend has a quick temper that always gets him into trouble. So he asks you about it. If you say, "Yeah, you're a major impatient pain in the backside," that will probably not help him. It will cut down his confidence. So instead, you should say something like this:

I think you have a great way of understanding people and you give good advice. This is a useful quality. Not many have it, and it is unfortunate if somebody doesn't explore it to the fullest because they simply don't have the patience to listen. But luckily, patience can be learned if there's a desire. So if you feel impatient sometimes, just work on it, and I'm sure you'll improve.

This way you didn't criticize your friend; instead, you made him feel his flaw can be corrected. Also you gave him a compliment, but still delivered your message. You didn't lie, but you weren't rude either.

It may seem unpleasant to give or receive a negative opinion, but it certainly is rewarding in the long run. You get to know others' boundaries as well as your own. Saying no from time to time helps us develop harmonious relationships. Practice saying no without saying the word "no." It takes time, and sometimes it is difficult, but is worth the effort.

Chapter 7: Be Selfish

In today's society, the word "selfish" has negative connotations. Selfish people follow their own self-interest and only their own self-interest. They don't care about the damage they do. They use others for their own benefit and to serve themselves. This is more or less the description of a selfish person, right?

But you can be selfish *and* help make other people happy. These two things aren't mutually exclusive. What's more, we can't make anybody else happy until we've satisfied our own needs. Before we learn how to be selfish and make others happy at the same time, we have to redefine the word "selfish."

Being considered selfish doesn't feel good, but acting selfishly can actually make you a better person, psychologists say. Melissa Deuter, a clinical assistant professor of psychiatry at the University of Texas Health Science Center at San Antonio, says, "You take responsibility for getting your personal, emotional and physical needs met, and that's an important part of becoming an adult."

Selfishness is being interested in your own needs and goals first, then in others'. If you feel like people step all over you and your head is full of chatter about what others want you to do for them, it's time to stop and think about how you feel about this exploitation. Becoming self-focused instead of self-involved will change your life drastically. You'll be happier, have healthier relationships, and be healthier too.

Two psychologists, Jonathan Berman and Deborah Small of the University of Pennsylvania, wrote and entire study on this subject entitled *Self-interest without Selfishness: The hedonic benefit of imposed self-interest*. They made tests to examine when people feel the happiest. The tests were then performed on undergraduate students. Each of them got three dollars, but one third of them were told to donate it to charity, one third were told to keep it for themselves, and one third could choose what they wanted to do with it.

The happiest group happened to be those students who were told to keep the money. "Often what people really want to do is act in a selfish manner. But they don't do that, because they know they will feel selfish if they do," said Mr. Berman.

In other words, people often feel guilty if they act selfishly. Altruism and self-sacrifice are highly admired concepts — however, they don't make the individual truly satisfied. So how can we be selfish, avoid guilt, and actually be good to others?

Satisfy yourself first, then try to make others happy and satisfied. Just like on airplanes, put on your oxygen mask first, then help those around you. If you are not happy, you can't honestly make others happy, and you can't help anyone without feeling negatively about it.

My grandmother, may she rest in peace, was the most self-sacrificing person I have ever known. She cooked for us, cleaned after us, and resigned from her hobbies to be able to meet our daily needs better and quicker. Do you think she was happy? No, she wasn't. She was constantly complaining about her unhappy and exploited life. A day didn't go by without her fantasizing about her death, or just remarking on how unfair life is. The worst part was that she didn't realize that nobody had asked for her sacrifice. She chose to do everything for us. Of course, it was more comfortable to let her do everything, but at the same time, we felt sorry for her, and our moods were poisoned as soon as she opened her mouth. My family tried to help her out, but she resisted.

Did she live her life for us? Yes. Was she happy? No. Were we happy? Not really.

Somehow she got comfortable in her martyrdom. She felt useful, irreplaceable. She did everything, but she demanded attention in a loud and emotionally blackmailing manner afterward. She wasn't feeling good enough unless she felt useful. My grandmother tried everything to live up to the conventional icon of selflessness, and she crippled herself in the process.

Her story illustrates how harmful compulsive selflessness can be. But was it true selflessness? She made all her sacrifices in order to feel good about herself and to legitimize her demands for attention. In fact, my grandma acted selfishly, but covertly.

Now I ask again: Is it really that flawed to benefit yourself first? Isn't it better to seek your fulfillment and *then* share joyous moments with others, rather than raging all day while stepping on yourself?

Put yourself first, then take care of others. In that order, not skipping either part. If you leave the second part — taking care of others — out of the equation, that's indeed a self-absorbed, unhealthy form of being selfish.

It's okay to say no.

Everything presented in the previous chapter can be applied here too. Saying no is a form of choosing yourself first. You don't have to do it in an obnoxious or hostile manner. Simply mention another commitment and say when you will fulfill the asker's request.

If you are sure you don't want to do it, make that clear in a friendly manner. Let's say a friend asks for a Buffett-worthy loan. Just tell your friend you'd love to help, but as a rule, you never lend money to friends. If you mention this general "excuse," you won't make your friend feel untrustworthy, your friendship won't suffer if this person doesn't pay the money back, and you won't be known to your friends as a two-legged ATM. Lending money is a sensitive prospect. Some people forgive any offense easier than the one against their wallet.

How to be a good selfish person when it comes to your family.

Let's say your cousin who lives in Hawaii invites you to her annual hula party for the eighth year in a row. You really don't want to pay for another trip to Hawaii, mostly because you've already "been there, done that" a couple of times.

If you want to skip the invitation, tell her as soon as possible. Although you had a lot of fun before, you won't be able to make it this year because your schedule is very busy. Do not tell her yes, then cancel at the last moment. Better get through the rejection quickly.

This way your cousin can't be angry with you. If you put the emphasis on your work schedule, then nobody can blame you. If you want to express your true appreciation for your cousin's invitation, send her a handwritten letter about missing her and attach a photo of you two doing some crazy hula stuff together. You may have been selfish, but you didn't hurt anybody.

How can you play the selfish card successfully at your workplace?

Let's say there is a new receptionist or intern at your company who hangs out on Facebook all the time. Your boss asks you to supervise her. Of course you don't want to engage in a war of the words with a teenager who has a social media crisis every other minute, but you don't want to say no to your boss either.

The only solution is to make your boss think you are more needed elsewhere. Tell your boss that you are interested in helping youngsters spread their wings, then add that you are very busy with such and such a project, but you'd gladly re-prioritize your tasks if your boss wants you to. This way you didn't say no, but you put the decision on your boss' shoulders.

If he really insists you check on the new colleague, squeeze it into your schedule. But if the amount of extra work is seriously hindering your other projects, ask for an appointment with your boss so you can redefine your work description and renegotiate your salary.

Being selfless can be the action of someone with low self-confidence getting other people's approval. Overcoming the fear of saying no to somebody and simply voting for yourself for the first time are both self-esteem-boosting actions.

Saying no will not only help you build confidence, but also:

Make you happier.

By making time to do what you love, or spending time with people you want, you become unquestionably happier.

Make you healthier.

If you are selfish, you tend to take better care of yourself. Don't spend your energy serving everyone else's needs. Serve your own. Exercise every day, and eat better for the sole reason of self-respect.

You will find your relationships improving.

Setting your limits and knowing others' limits and respecting them is an integral part of developing good relationships. People can't take advantage of you so easily if you are selfish. And as for romantic relationships, if you look for somebody to fill your gaps and end up subordinating yourself, you won't have a balanced and happy romance. If two adults with clear needs and boundaries meet and enjoy each other, it can be an A+ match.

Being selfish doesn't mean being egoistical and reckless. Don't burn bridges or act crazy-selfish and me-centric from one day to the next. Just follow the rule: "I take care of myself first, and then I take care of others."

To pursue your goals, you need comrades. If you make people think you're egotistical, your life won't be better. Find a balance where your acts of selfishness are inspiring and respectable, not unappealing. If you don't forget about the "help others" part, there's little chance you'd end up on the negative side of the scale.

Chapter 8: Leave The Past In The Past

What are you holding onto? What's holding you back? Is it an old offense, a relationship that doesn't work?

Do you have a best friend from childhood? Did you make sandcastles and have sleepovers where you put on Barbie fashion shows? But today, somehow, things just aren't the same. Your friend is a devoted lawyer, and you are a creative-minded web designer, and you guys just don't live in the same world anymore.

However, for the sake of the old days, you get together and spend ten minutes telling each other what you did in the past year. Then you spend another ten minutes sharing nostalgic memories before the awkward silence falls between you. Both of you feel these encounters unnecessary and weird but, because of guilt, you keep having them.

This example is a mild one. People keep others in their lives for much less legit reasons than childhood memories.

Here are some common examples of relationships and conditions you should consider letting go of.

Growing apart from somebody.

Sometimes we evolve away from each other as our core values change. What's the first step you need to take to let these relationships go?

First and foremost, accept the changeability of human nature. It's nobody's fault if you grew apart from someone dear. Probably the other person feels the same about you.

Secondly, if you don't hold onto this relationship in a forced manner, it will fade naturally. You'll meet every five years at graduation anniversaries, and you can discuss what happened during those years. Maybe you'll find out that there are again common grounds you can talk about — you both have a family, children, and a common hobby. Who knows? But don't try to force something that is not going well at the moment.

Not letting go of an old grudge.

If somebody has hurt you, cheated on you, or mistreated you, holding onto your anger will harm only one person — you. It will keep you from other opportunities and steal away a lot of your energy.

Are you afraid to let go of the past? What are you afraid of? Are you simply afraid that if you let fear go, you'll find something good? Something you could have had much sooner if you had let bygones be bygones?

A happy ending.

There is a saying that in the end, you'll reach happiness. If you are not happy yet, this means it's not the end of that particular event. Life is about learning, and the miracle is the journey, not the destination. Sometimes we focus so much on the happiness of the endgame that we forget to appreciate the gifts life gives us on the way there.

Your needs and goals have changed.

You change just like the seasons, the moon, and nature. It is natural. So stop feeling guilty if something you wanted four years ago doesn't apply anymore. Acknowledging the need to start over requires real power.

Do you feel frustrated about something?

Cry it out — loudly and openly. If you keep it in, it can manifest as physical illness. Engage in a new positive activity. Learn a new skill or exercise. Turning your focus to something new and pleasurable can help build a bridge between a bitter past and promising future.

Are you angry?

Don't try to avoid this feeling. It's better to feel it fully. Talk to the people who hurt you after the first waves of rage have passed. If you try to hide it or hold it in, it will inevitably burst out and may hurt innocent people. Remind yourself that nothing lasts forever, and neither will your anger. Try to understand what triggered this anger, how can you defuse it, and where your responsibility lies in accepting the anger.

Are past relationships holding you back?

Yes, emotional bonds are the hardest to break. However, your relationship reached this point for a reason. Try to un-romanticize this bond and face the facts. Make an unbiased list of good and bad things you've experienced in this relationship. It will help you to see if more things weigh on the negative side, many of which were probably the reason the relationship ended in the first place.

There are always bigger fish ... and there is always a better love. Don't make the mistake of convincing yourself that nobody will love you as much as the other person did. Do your best to love yourself as much as possible. When you learn to love yourself, you won't need as much emotional validation from others.

Loving yourself starts with letting go. First, let go of guilt. Trust yourself and know that when the rain stops the sun will come out. It always does.

In ancient India, a girl asked her father to give her a birthday gift that would raise her spirit in times of sorrow, and bring her back to Earth when she was head over heels. The father acknowledged her request. For her birthday, he gave her a medal with three words engraved upon its surface: "Nothing lasts forever."

If you accept this truth, you'll be less fearful and your life, and thus your social interactions will be more balanced. If you acknowledge the inevitability of good and bad in life, you won't get stuck or paralyzed by fear. What has to happen will happen whether you stress about it or not.

After acceptance comes forgiveness. You have to forgive others for your sake and your peace of mind. If you hold your bitterness inside, you poison yourself without proving a thing to your wrongdoer. You'll only destroy yourself. Maybe that person doesn't even know how much she hurt you. If she knows but didn't make it up to you, then maybe she hurt you on purpose and your bitterness will only make her perversely gleeful that she succeeded. So forgive, let go, and live worry-, grudge-, and regret-free.

Chapter 9: Conversation Chameleon

Do you know somebody who is always the heart of the conversation? Who can exchange a few good words with geeks, then jump right in with the fancy people, and then talk to the hard rock lovers? Does this person understand everybody? How?

Is this person a mentalist, polymath, language expert, and subculture scientist all at the same time?

I call these types of people "conversation chameleons" because they can change the color of their conversation all the time. Color, in this sense, is their way of approaching people, their intonation, the topics they talk about, the language they use, and their body language.

These five points are the keys to their success. Conversation chameleons are not polymaths, but they are excellent observers and are naturally interested in others.

Would you like to become a conversation chameleon too? Then follow the next five steps.

The way of approaching.

This is the most important step. The way you approach is everything you don't notice your chameleon friend doing because it all happens before the conversation actually starts. A conversation chameleon always does his "homework." What do I mean, exactly?

He selects the people or person he wants to connect with. First, he doesn't talk to them — just observes how they interact with other people and each other. He keeps a mental note about it.

Afterward, the conversation chameleon observes how others react to this person or group. For example, people may be afraid of the hard rock lovers because they have a specific way of dressing up and manifesting publicly. If you want rock lovers to like or respect you, do not show fear. This is stereotyping, of course. I also like hard rock and look nothing like a true fan. The example is illustrative, but you get the gist.

Beware stereotyping in general. Putting someone in a box is the easiest way to make him or her hostile toward you. Since I travel frequently, I run into lots of stereotypes people have toward Eastern Europeans in different countries. I'm not saying that the stereotypes exist for no reason, but it's very discouraging when someone judges me based on a stereotype that doesn't apply to me. Naturally, those people will occupy the lowest positions on my "love list." Why should I like someone who judges me prematurely and unjustly based on generalizations?

Some people try to approach certain groups based on negative stereotypes. They think negative stereotypes are funny, and they want to break the ice by making fun of a negative stereotype. Still, they probably will thicken that proverbial ice between them and the group. Positive stereotypes can backfire as well, so just forget about stereotypes. Find another point of connection that is specific for that particular group you want to approach.

Try to find a topic your chosen group finds interesting and intrigues you too. This way, you'll have a point of connection. Casually mention some information they can ask more about. For example, if traveling is the main interest of the group, you can say something like, "When I was traveling, I made the most hilarious discovery: the thing I miss the most from home are the restroom conditions."

This is a gutsy, funny statement that opens the door to many questions. Where were you traveling when you made this discovery? What's the story? What else do you miss when you travel? Where are the worst toilets, where are the best? Etc.

If you're lucky, the foundation of the relationship can be established right there, but let's say that something goes wrong, whether they have to rush somewhere, they are not in the best mood, or the interaction breaks. Still, they know who you are and from now on, you can smile and say "hi" when you see them. They will remember and eventually start approaching you too.

Intonation.

Steps two through five can be called "mirroring steps." This means you adjust to others' frequencies like a radio — you have to be on a particular wavelength to catch the perfect broadcast. If you are a bit higher or lower, the reception will be bad. If you are on a totally different wavelength, you won't receive anything from the desired radio station.

So, intonation. There is always a certain level of tension in a person's voice and from that, you can tell if that person is calm, excited, scared, or indifferent. If someone uses a very scared tone, don't use your most badass, aggressive tone, otherwise you'll scare that person off. If your conversation partner has a harsh, annoyed tone, don't bring out your highest-pitched, mouse-like tone. Talk confidently. If someone has the tone of a bully, it is not smart to try to be an even bigger bully. Stay calm and confident. The situation always reveals the right intonation to use. Pay attention and you'll notice.

Topics to talk about.

After doing your field research, you can do some follow-up work on Google. Let's say you made sure that your hard rock lover group likes to talk about motorcycles. While conducting your research, you'll see that the next motorbike festival is coming up soon. Look up different motorcycles, choose which one you really like, and read up on its features so when you engage in the conversation and they ask you about your favorite, you have an actual answer instead of saying something like, "Umm, oh, the ones with two wheels."

If you already started talking, try to recall stories from your life that resemble the stories of the speaker. This way you can create rapport. You can relate to others and they can relate to you.

For example, Klaus says something about his boss, who he doesn't like. It turns out the guy is a narcissistic psycho. This thought of a narcissistic psycho triggers a memory from your own life from when your father was still alive and made a very harsh accusation about you.

So you decide to share the story about your dad with Klaus. You mention that your relationship with your dad was a good lesson in learning how to deal with narcissists later in life. Your story reminds Klaus of a good joke about how women shut down narcissistic men. He tells you and you have a good laugh. The joke reminds you of a situation when in a comedy club the comedian was struggling with his jokes, but he couldn't make you laugh half as much as Klaus did.

And it goes on and on as a good conversation should.

Language.

The more time you spend interacting with your chosen group, the more you'll understand their verbal and non-verbal communication. If you want to feel you truly belong to a group, you have to learn how they talk about things. When you hear an uncommon term like slang or jargon, just make note of it in your memory and use it the next time that topic pops up.

Every group has their little inside jokes — like words that identify them and make them different from others. Try to catch these words as soon as possible and incorporate them into your vocabulary. This vocabulary assimilation eventually would happen anyway, but the sooner you start to act like one of the group, the sooner you'll be accepted as one of them.

Body language.

Last but not least is body language. Mirroring in body language means scanning the other person to see if they gesture or move as you do. In our case, after the observation, you should adopt the gestures of the group. By mirroring them you are saying, "Look at me, I'm just the same as you." By mirroring you create rapport and a sense of bonding, which will most likely help you be accepted.

Being in sync with somebody starts early, when you are in the womb of your mother and your heartbeats' are synchronized. When somebody says they have the right vibes with you, they are subconsciously referring to mirroring.

If you take into consideration the five points above, you'll develop excellent conversational skills very quickly. However, I'd like to draw your attention to a few "danger zones" where even the best can fall from time to time.

Always keep the option open that you may have read a person wrong. Humans are moody creatures. Maybe the day of your observation was a bad day. This is why it is crucial not to make final verdicts based on one or two occasions.

People are generally nice, but they can behave obnoxiously for personal reasons. If your first attempt at speaking to someone is a failure, give them at least one more try. They will probably apologize if they are genuinely nice people just having a bad day. If this doesn't happen and you talk through each other again, accept that sometimes people don't click. It is rare, but it happens.

If, after a few conversations, you realize you don't like the group or person, try to keep your distance. If they call you over, try to use topics that are of little interest. Suddenly made interest can fade just as quickly as it is created. However, don't stop talking or saying hi to them. Simply step out of the clique.

Last but not least, I'd like to add something very important to avoid misunderstandings.

When being a conversation chameleon, you don't have to let go of your true colors. You shouldn't wear a different mask for every group. Wearing masks is not sustainable, nor is it credible. Stay the same person and adjust some of your very basic surface manifestations. Your identity should stay the same, and you can show your new friends how much more there is inside you.

Chapter 10: How to Handle Difficult Conversations

Even if you are a good communicator, there will always be some conversations you wish you could avoid. Some may be unpleasant for a variety of reasons, like the following:

- You don't like the person you are talking to.

- Some things must be said — and you have to be the criticizer.

- You are being criticized.

What's the solution to these problems?

In the first case when you don't like the person you have to talk to, just think about that person as another human being. They are human just like you, and just like you, they hate to be treated unfairly and spoken badly of. So when it comes to sorting things out with someone you dislike, try to act as you would like to be treated.

Of course, it depends on the issue you are facing. If you need to talk to your girlfriend who just cheated on you, or your broker who just tricked you into an unprofitable investment, it is more difficult to stay cool and objective. I could write (and probably will) an entire book about how to handle these complex, highly emotional conversations, but now let's just stick with the smelly coworker or loud neighbor examples.

Be objective, quick, and state your clear wishes or affirmations.

If you must be critical, the best advice I can give you is from Dale Carnegie's book *How to Win Friends and Influence People*. Begin by praising and appreciating people. There must be something about that person you can compliment. If people hear a positive remark first, they tend to accept criticism more easily. They won't feel like an unworthy person, but like a human who has virtues and flaws.

If people feel important in your eyes, they will be

more eager to correct their mistakes. If they only feel scolded all the time, you'll achieve the opposite of what you actually want. Their will to improve will decrease. They will only have feelings of contempt and anger toward you.

It's even better if you call attention to their mistakes indirectly. For example, let's say your secretary left some typos in the annual report.

Instead of screaming, "Can't you write?!" say something like, "Good summary of the main achievements of the company. However, I'd appreciate if you'd read it through once again to make sure everything is correct."

You can give that look of *I'm the boss, and I know*, and your secretary will give you back a look of *I know — and I know that you know that I know*. Then the secretary will diligently review the report and be grateful for your tolerance. Most likely, she will be more precise next time and make sure there are no more typos.

When you are the one who is criticized, that's a tough situation to handle calmly because when people are criticized, their most natural reaction is to deny the accusation. Most often, they don't let their guards down even when they know they're wrong. The most annoying scenario is when you're criticized unfairly. This is even harder to digest than fair criticism. But if somebody complains about your quick temper and you react by lashing out, screaming, "I'm not quick-tempered!" you'll only prove their point.

There are a lot of options for how to handle criticism, but since this book is about improving your social charisma, I'll share the peaceful, smart solutions. This approach won't burn bridges, but rather smoothens things out.

First step:

Don't say "you're wrong" to anybody. Even to a critic. Even if he's wrong. Just as you found their criticism offensive, they will feel offended by your counter-attack. If you want to change the flow of the conversation, you need to respond smartly rather than by taking a hard negotiation stance.

Answer someone's criticism or provocation in an unexpected way. When criticizing, people expect a harsh defense. Don't pick a fight, but instead, stay calm. This way, you'll surprise your conversation partner. They will fall out of their secure position as the critic and face a situation they were not prepared for.

You can say something like, "I agree with you. There are occasions when I make this mistake. Please tell me how I offended you so I can apologize and make sure not make that same mistake again."

Opportunities for argument will be gone. If people do in fact tell you about times you've offended your accuser, then apologize and truly try to not do it again.

If someone's wrong about something — let's say they quoted something wrong — don't be quick on correcting him. Choose your battles wisely. There are mistakes that are worth picking a fight over and trying to correct them — something of great stakes like a final report or serious misconduct — but most mistakes people make are so irrelevant that you should give a second thought as to whether it is worth pointing out. You may be right. But people don't like to be wrong. If your goal is to increase your likability, becoming the office's smart-ass is not the best place to start.

Second step:

Try to see the story from the other person's point of view. Separate impact from intent. When you were criticized and found it unfair, find out why that person spoke up. Tell them you accept that they feel this way, although it's not entirely clear why. Ask them to tell you so you understand their viewpoint better. Most of the time, the parties miscommunicate. If your critique was right about what he said, you may learn some great lessons on how to improve.

Third step:

If your critic was right about what she said, admit it quickly and apologize if necessary. Admitting and taking responsibility for your mistakes is a sign of maturity. This way, even your enemy will respect you for having a strong backbone and the courage to accept your flaws.

Handling misunderstandings with blame, arguments, and a self-centered attitude won't do you any good. You'll never truly win an argument. If you lose, you've lost. If you win, you may lose the other person's goodwill. Unless you want to live alone, you need people's goodwill.

Embrace confrontations:

Confrontation has a negative connotation. There are those battles, however, which you have to engage in. It is necessary to protect and maintain your own boundaries and values. This doesn't mean you have to step on the boundaries and values of others; you should respect those too. But if you feel yours have been stepped on, you have to step up and honestly talk about it. Especially with those closest to you. Confrontation is often painful, but it is a necessary pain that in the long-term builds intimacy and facilitates healthy relationships.

If you are full of shame and anxiety, you can become obsessed with living up to others' expectations. But in the long-term, this kind of approach to life cripples your soul.

As soon as you let yourself to be seen as vulnerable, open up about your shame, and undertake some confrontation, if necessary, to protect your identity, you'll suddenly feel relieved. If you do these things, you'll realize that it is much more uncomfortable to deny your own expectations than the expectations of others.

Once you discover the liberating power of honesty, you won't feel the need to say what you think others want to hear in order to protect their feelings.

The first few times you speak your mind or protect your values, you'll feel a bit confused. On one hand, you'll feel liberated, but on the other hand, you'll feel like you're a selfish person. Remember, selfishness is good as long as you take care of others after yourself. This is how being honest with yourself starts — you set your boundaries and live up to them.

Pick your battles wisely. If someone is not worth the confrontation, don't engage. Let it go. You don't need to prove any point to strangers. If your honesty and boundaries repel some people around you, let them go. Those who truly love you will respect your boundaries and stick around. Moreover, you'll attract the right people into your life. Your kind of people — who are not afraid to be honest and who have similar values as you. Honesty opens you up to express gratitude and appreciation more easily. Showing true gratitude and value to people is also beneficial in building charisma.

Chapter 11: Be Tough Instead of Rude

Some people try to hide their lack of confidence by acting rudely, but you can see a clear difference between real and fake confidence. Real confidence radiates and is intimidating and inspiring at the same time. It is never loud, exhibitionist, or repressive because a person with real confidence knows these actions are not necessary. People who are confident don't need to prove they are.

On the other hand, those with fake confidence are boastful, overly self-assured, and sometimes even aggressive with their opinions. All this gives them an obnoxious air. They have the typical "I want people to fear me instead of like me" attitude. But unless you are Machiavelli reborn or you are a king with an empire to hold together, making people fear you will do you no good.

Even though truly confident people are generally friendly, they also have to draw a line somewhere to protect their boundaries. When they do, other people consider them tough, but not rude. How is it possible to protect your interests firmly, but also kindly?

Prioritize. I'm sure that even the most patient person on Earth has a daily tolerance level, which when exceeded makes the person rude instead of fair. Thus, we have to learn to prioritize the people we don't want to offend under any circumstances.

People tend to be more patient with strangers and less patient with people they are friends with. When it comes to family, people usually stand on one side of two extremes: either they are indulgent and never follow through (the classic case of spoiled children), or they always release their tension onto close relatives (wife, husband, mother, father, kid, etc.).

I'm sure you don't want to hurt your family or friends intentionally, but when your daily tolerance level is exceeded, you can do two things. One, you can improve your tolerance level and patience skills — this is a long journey, but highly recommended. Or you can prioritize whom will you be patient with.

For example, if you must lash out at someone it better be the rude saleslady, the delivery guy who was thirty minutes late, or another stranger. I'm not saying you should do this. Strive to become more patient in general. But if you *must* erupt, it is better to take things out on a stranger who you'll never see again than it is your loved ones.

Decide what kind of person you want to be. Do you want to be known as someone who is hysterical and crackles like water on oil, or someone patient and caring without being taken advantage of? But how do you stay patient and caring when there are so many challenging situations?

It is difficult to stay in the moment when tension is rising. Sometimes you come back to the present only when you've already carried out your anger, and you're ready to burn everything around you.

1. How can you be tough without being rude to your family?

If your kid is nagging you for their hundredth Barbie doll, you have to draw a line. I mean, you should have done it like ninety-eight Barbie dolls before, but you have to start somewhere. Tell your kid, kindly but firmly, that you disapprove of her behavior. But never make her feel unloved. So start like this:

You know that I love you very much, but ...

Do not threaten her, just simply explain why she doesn't need a new doll and how badly her conduct is affecting you.

If you have to draw boundaries for you parents or spouse, start the same way:

I love you very much, and I know you love me. And maybe you are not aware, but with this behavior and words, you hurt me and make me feel uncomfortable. Was this your intention?

There is a good chance your parents or spouse won't say yes, they wanted to hurt you. Instead, they will probably say no, of course not. You made them realize that they were not treating you well. Now it is their responsibility to change their hurtful ways.

2. How do you balance toughness and kindness with others?

Let's say we're talking about a friend of yours. If they do something that makes you feel bad, as a first step, you can explain the situation the same way I suggested you speak to your family above. You should let them know how and why they hurt you. However, if it happens a second time, you may have to remind your friend more firmly to stop. You don't have to be rude in this case either. Rudeness doesn't bring results anyway.

Simply point out that if the person doesn't stop the disturbing behavior, you will leave and discuss the matter later when you are both calmer. At this point, it is critical to keep your word. Get up and leave if the person doesn't stop. Don't forget to mention that you are still open to discussing this issue when the person is ready to approach things differently.

The main points here are tranquility, lack of rudeness, lack of aggression, and consistency.

Toughening your heart from time to time and respecting your own boundaries won't make you a less likable person. On the contrary, you will exhibit truly confident charisma. To achieve this, there is no need for ugly words or fights. Simply know your boundaries and your daily tolerance level, and make it clear to others.

You can always work on expanding your boundaries and learn to be more patient, but you live in the here and now, and you have to make your current limits known and respected to enjoy happy and healthy relationships.

Chapter 12: Respect Must Be Earned

Let me start with a personal story about my ex-boss, who was the manager of our company. Objectively speaking, she was a good worker She was diligent and hard-working, but nobody respected her. I could even say everyone hated her. Why? Because she was rude, condescending, and she loved to publicly humiliate her subordinates. Even so, she forced everyone to respect her. She demanded it. If that didn't happen, she retaliated with punishments.

Respect is one of the most powerful human emotions. We can earn the respect of anyone, even of those who don't particularly like us. We often hear people say they respect their enemies, so respect doesn't even require love.

How can you make yourself respected without demanding it? In the following pages, I'll give you ten ideas for how to quickly boost your respect in another person's eyes.

Making demands will never earn you respect, but honesty and sincerity can. If others feel you're speaking from your heart and that you will stand behind your words, beliefs, and actions, you'll be regarded as a person to be trusted and respected. Learn to be sincere with your friends at work, and in all parts of your life.

Give to get. This applies to respect too. There are many ways you can show your respect for another person.

Listen to them instead of interrupting after every second sentence because you have something to add about yourself. If you want to earn someone's respect quickly, learn to listen actively — ask questions and summarize their story. People feel interesting when they are asked to talk about themselves.

Follow up your conversations. For example, if somebody tells you she has a difficult exam on

Friday, you can text her after the exam. This will mark you as an attentive person and a thoughtful friend who takes time to remember and ask.

Be empathetic. Pay attention when somebody tells you he's fine, but doesn't seem so. Lend a shoulder and listen to his emotional needs. You can earn his respect and be thought of as a caring, thoughtful person who is attentive to the needs of others.

Stay tuned. Connect with your friends and family. Update them on your latest life events and ask about theirs.

Treat others as you want to be treated. It is called the Golden Rule for a reason. Respect starts only when you respect yourself.

Keep your promises, otherwise you will be considered a person of words, not one of actions, and a person of words is less likely to be respected. Keep a "promise diary" if you know you tend to forget stuff. I do. I don't like to promise many things, but if I do promise something, I instantly enter it into my promise diary with the person's name to whom I promised it. I also write the details of the promise if there are any, like the deadline, who I should contact, etc.

Don't waste other people's time. Others will respect your time if you do the same for them. This means being punctual for appointments, meetings, and even brunch. Don't spend your time talking about useless things. In business, get to the point fast and help make decisions easy for others. Time is a precious thing, so respect yourself and others by not wasting it.

Stand up for yourself and others. Stop dealing with people mistreating you. Be diplomatic and act like a professional, but not a mute one. Speaking up for yourself in a charming, yet serious manner is hard to do, and this is why it is considered to be an action that deserves respect.

This statement also applies to when you see injustice around you. You don't have to pretend to be almighty, but you shouldn't ignore ill deeds, either. It is better to avoid confrontations, but sometimes, there is no choice. There may be occasions when you need to stand up for others, especially when they cannot stand up for themselves.

Don't think about anything offensive when I say stand up for yourself. You can simply ask, "Based on what facts do you say this about me or that person?" This way, you ask for an explanation. If the offender has a good reason, he'll probably tell you. You can decide whether or not it is true. If it is, be quick to say sorry and move on. If he is not right, he probably won't have any argument. Instead, he'll say something like, "Because I said so," and most likely will retreat.

Practice being humble. It is a highly under-appreciated quality in today's society, yet most big role models are humble. If Warren Buffett, Steve Jobs, or the Pope can be humble, why wouldn't you?

Don't look down on those who are not as wealthy or well-educated as you are. It doesn't mean they can't teach you something. You can learn from everybody and everything. You can learn even from a haulm that stays strong, swaying in the hurricane while the tallest trees are torn from the ground.

Offer your help to others, but avoid being a brownnoser. Volunteer from time to time for something nobody wants to do, or help someone who didn't ask for your help but obviously needs it.

However, distinguish kindness from being a busybody who always has something to do for people. If you're too helpful all the time, people may think you're a compulsive pleaser. Being too nice is a bad policy if your goal is to be respected.

Inspire. The most respected people are usually those who inspire others to achieve great things. Smiling, staying on the sunny side, positively remarking on any improvement of others, assuring them that they can reach their dreams if they work hard for them — these are all small gestures that don't cost you a thing, but can brighten someone's day.

Improve your sense of humor. People who take themselves too seriously usually achieve the opposite effect: They are considered funny, but in a bad way. A healthy sense of humor and the ability to laugh at your own mistakes are traits essential to earning respect.

Remember Jennifer Lawrence's epic fall at the Oscar gala? Was it a challenging moment for her? Sure thing. But how did she handle it? By making fun of herself, not by blaming the dress designer, the red carpet maker, or air conditioning devices for her lost balance.

Strength of character isn't only about believing in yourself, but also about having the courage to admit when you messed up. Nobody is perfect, so you shouldn't worry too much. Take responsibility for your actions. If you start something, finish it. If you agree to a task, do it. Be trustworthy. If you are engaged in a project when you encounter some extra tasks you didn't take into consideration, do not quit. Don't go to your boss with bloodshot eyes and complain. Instead, take a moment to calm down and check to see if you can complete the extra tasks alone. If not, ask for advice and help. Speaking confidently and honestly about your issues and seeking help isn't shameful. Quitting is.

Do not forget that respect is a fragile bond; it goes as easily as it comes. If you invest many years into gaining respect, don't lose your hard work with one reckless and foolish action.

Chapter 13: Deepen and Open

By this point, you've read about how to become a better storyteller, how to earn respect in your social life, how to keep confrontations on the constructive side, and how to relate in the best way possible to a group you wish to join. If you pay attention to what's been said in the book so far and practice the exercises, like the one of improvisation or the one which improves your storytelling skills, you'll notice an improvement in your communication ability.

The more you practice these exercises with real people, the more you'll actually deepen your relationship with them. The more stories, experiences, and ideas you share and relate to others, the better you'll get to know the person in question, and the deeper the bond between you will become.

Since I left college a few years ago and have my own business, I've been feeling that creating deep, quality relationships isn't so easy like it was in the school. If you think back to your college or high school years, you'll see how much easier it was to establish friendships compared to now. School offered a constant meeting point, a similar life situation, and similar memory background. All you had to do was to open your mouth and say something. Chances were high that ninety percent of your classmates could relate with what you said.

After we leave school, everything becomes more heterogenic — the people you meet at work don't necessarily share the same reality as you. They did not have sleepless nights because of Mrs. Briggs, the heartless math teacher. How to create depth when you share no common past you could start a conversation about?

At a workplace, the best way to "find friends" is to create a common reality. In your case, the first chunk of talking probably should be about your company, the job, and what you like and dislike doing. Try to avoid talking about who you like or dislike. Gossiping may backfire.

The next time you meet this person, take the conversation to a deeper level. Ask about your coworkers' previous work experience. What did she like about that job, and what did he hate? Don't ask questions that require a yes or no answer.

For example, if you ask, "Did you like your old job?" you'll get a yes or a no. If your conversation partner is a shy talker, chances are that the conversation will stick in the mud. To go on, you'll need to make an extra effort. It's better to ask, "What did you like or hate the most about your past job? Do you have a fun story?" In this case, the person is sort of cornered to respond with a story. Pay attention to the story, and based on what it was about, relate to it with a story from your own past workplace.

Be careful, though. Don't try to overdo your conversation partner with your story. There are some obnoxious people who always know better, who always had a better shot, a bigger loss, or a greater motorcycle accident, and who can always trump the stories of others.

So tell a story that's similar to your conversation partner's. With the resolution of the story, you can take the conversation one layer deeper. For example, your story was about how your boss tied your hands all the time and bound the creative genius inside you. This topic brings up the perfect opportunity to take the idea of creativity repression to the general field. You can talk about how much it frustrates you when someone tries to repel creativity. You can mention that you consider yourself very free-spirited.

Your conversation partner might relate to that by telling you that her father is just the same. You can ask if she likes this particular trait in her father. She will answer by briefly explaining her weird relationship with her free-spirited father and conservative mother ...

You see? From workplace to daddy issues in twenty minutes. This is a short, by-the-book way to get to know people and establish connections and rapport. It's nothing awfully complicated; just detecting small topics that can deepen and further the conversation. Not everybody can be led into a deep conversation so quickly. Sooner or later, you can establish rapport even with the shyest, most withdrawn person. It depends on your persistence and sensibility when asking questions, and choosing well your stories you wish to relate to them with.

Every person has a surface level side and a deeper side. Each relationship starts by scratching the surface. Surface level topics are hobbies, animals, music, workplace, physical traits, food, school, etc. I wouldn't advise starting a relationship on divisive surface level topics as religion, politics, or beliefs in general. When the surface is scratched, find a way to get deeper into the person's head and soul. Deeper topics are family relationships, romantic relationships, ambitions, dreams, beliefs, fears, insecurities, hopes … The deep topics create the real emotional experience based on if we decide to deepen the relationship further or not. Deep conversations trigger empathy, sympathy, curiosity, or attraction.

Loving the same music or playing the same instrument are not legitimate reasons to become friends or lovers. Those are just superficialities. Sharing similar beliefs, hopes for the future, visions, or worldviews is more likely to create that kind of bond.

Connecting on a deeper level is never unidirectional. You have to share and be shared with to truly forge a bond. If you share but the other person doesn't, or vice versa, the relationship's quality won't deepen. The more personal the topics become, the more anxiety you'll feel to open up if you're not accustomed to talking about yourself on a deeper level. Creating friendships isn't only about going to watch the finals together or playing basketball in the courtyard. It is also about crying on each other's shoulders and talking about our greatest fears.

Social anxiety is rooted in feelings of inadequacy, shame, and fear. Opening up about your insecurities would mean bringing these deep-rooted phobias to surface. It's scary. But if you don't do it, your relationships won't deepen. It is a vicious cycle. The necessary step to deepen your relationships irritates your shame and feelings of unworthiness. It all depends on which wish is stronger in you: to establish better connections, or to hide your fears.

Talking about your fears is like working out a muscle group. The more you expose your fears, the more you'll confront them. Constantly challenging your social anxiety and acting against it will actually diminish your social anxiety. The first few occasions are hard as … a rock, but after that, it will become easier and easier.

Embrace your vulnerability.

The concept of vulnerability has been made well-known by Dr. Brene Brown. She talks about it in her books *Daring Greatly* and *Gifts of Imperfection*.

Vulnerability means admitting and embracing insecurities, sharing fears, and talking about things you never thought about talking before.

It means sharing memories that are embarrassing or which make you uncomfortable.

Brene Brown found that "the more people expose their shame, the more confident they become as a result." Social anxiety slowly vanishes and the obstacle removes itself from the way of having deeper and more robust connections.

Know that every time you decide to stay silent about a shame you carry — like binge-eating, being bullied in childhood, having an abusive parent, or feeling stupid — you miss the opportunity to get closer to solving it. Opening up about the issues mentioned above creates sympathy in the listener and releases a lot of tension from your shoulders.

Believe it or not, our imperfections are what draw us to one another. We relate to each other through our rough edges, not the smooth surfaces. Great intimacy comes with great insecurities trustingly shared.

Chapter 14: Fifty Points of Social Confidence

Being socially charismatic isn't innate. As you've learned in this book, it is composed of traits you pick up alongside the road and practice day by day, diligently and with a lot of self-awareness.

Below are the fifty main lessons from the previous chapters in bullet points so you can check them anytime you need a little reminder.

1. Do your research about the people you intend to speak with.
2. Talk with someone about the interests and habits of the group you want to join.
3. Two ears, one mouth — listen more, speak less.
4. Acknowledge that as you are on the inside, you will appear on the outside.
5. If you want people to like you, constant complaining won't help.

6. Claim the opposite of every negative self-label you ever think about or say aloud.

7. If a defeatist, negative, or self-deprecating thought develops in your head, quickly tell yourself STOP! STOP STOP STOP!

8. Let people like you for who you are.

9. Find the cause of your self-destructive monologues.

10. Don't say anything to yourself that you wouldn't say about your mother, your love, or your best friend.

11. Crush emotional spasms.

12. Learn to be humble.

13. False modesty is unlikable, just like boasting.

14. Being unsocial, in addition to dooming you to a lonely life, is physically unhealthy.

15. Stop being judgmental.

16. Stop labeling yourself as shy or antisocial.

17. List your positive qualities.

18. Stop over-analyzing your interactions.

19. People-pleasing is not attractive.

20. Think about how you can maximize your strengths and be socially likable at the same time.

21. Strengthen your improvising muscle.

22. Ask questions instead of giving direct comments.

23. Put away your phone.

24. Appeal to people's perceived selves.

25. Establish a role model.

26. Be the main and supporting actor at the same time.
27. Learn to say no.
28. Be selfish and help make others happy — these aren't mutually exclusive actions.
29. Do you feel frustrated about something? Cry it out — loudly and openly.
30. Are you angry? Don't try to avoid this feeling; rather, feel it fully.
31. There are always bigger fish ... and a better love.
32. Trust yourself and know that when the rain ends, the sun will come out.
33. Watch your intonation, your language, and body language.
34. When it comes to sorting out things with someone who you dislike, try to behave as you would like to be treated.
35. If you must be the criticizer, begin with praising and appreciating people's efforts.
36. Never say "you're wrong."
37. Answer in an unexpected way.
38. Try to see the story from the other person's point of view.
39. If your critic is right, admit it quickly and apologize if necessary.
40. Toughening your heart and respecting your own well-being and mental sanity won't make you a less

likable person.

41. Decide what kind of person you want to be.

42. Demanding words will never earn respect, but honest and sincere words can.

43. Keep your promises.

44. Don't waste other people's time.

45. Stand up for yourself and others.

46. Offer your help to others, but avoid being a brownnoser.

47. Humor is a weapon and a balm.

48. Inspire others.

49. Give respect to get it.

50. Don't give up.

I suggest you print these bullet points and keep them somewhere you can see them daily. Run through them quickly every day to memorize their main message so that you can instantly react to a situation by finding the right answer in your passive memory.

Remember, you won't become more charismatic just by reading them; you also need to apply them. It's up to you which advice you'll use. You have to know what areas of social interaction you want to improve upon. Maybe you will apply ten percent of the advice in this book, maybe ninety. I really hope I helped you with some thoughtful ideas.

"Charisma only wins people's attention. Once you have their attention, you have to have something to tell them."

—Daniel Quinn

Epilogue

Some say that true power is not physical, but rather, it is the power of the heart. Someone who decides to buy a book like this is devoted to change. If you set your desire to change deeply enough in your strong heart, there is nothing that can stop you!

I truly believe in the law of change. Everything changes around us — the seasons, the environment. And we are a part of nature, so we also change. Since change is inevitable, why not change for the better? It's in your hands. It's your choice.

I encourage you to find the willpower in yourself to follow your own path. The only person you can completely influence is you.

Be honest with yourself, trust your gut, and be charming, lively, and happy! Live your days as if they were your last! Go and charm the socks off everyone with your social charisma and lovable character!

I believe in you!

Yours truly,

Zoe

More Books By Zoe

Unbreakable Confidence
Build Grit
Find What You Were Born For – Book 1
Find What You Were Born For – Book 2
Find Who You Were Born To Be
Catching Courage
Fearless
Daily Routine Makeover
Daily Routine Makeover – Morning Edition
Less Mess Less Stress

www.ingramcontent.com/pod-product-compliance
Lightning Source LLC
Chambersburg PA
CBHW070248230526
45470CB00002B/529